I eat only white foods:

eggs, sugar, scraped bones, animal fat, veal, salt,

coconuts, chicken boiled in white water, fruit with mold, rice, turnips,

RYTHING
AINED

camphorized sausage, paste,

cheese (white), cotton salad, and certain

kinds of fish (without skin) . . . .

I breathe carefully, a little at a time. I rarely dance. When walking, I

hold my sides and keep my eyes fixed behind me.

I look very serious. If I laugh, it is not on purpose. Afterwards, I always

excuse myself nicely.

I sleep with one eye open; my sleep is very deep. My bed is round, with a

hole in the middle for my head . . . .

To my friends at Vermont College,
with gratitude and affection.

—M. T. A

To E.S.
—P. M.

Strange Mr. Satie

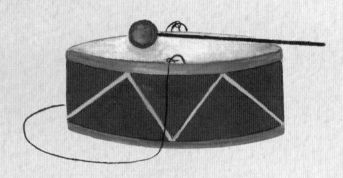

by

M. T. Anderson

illustrated by

Petra Mathers

VIKING

Erik Satie
was born by the sea
in the village of Honfleur
on the coast of France.
It was 1866.

"I was born
very young
in a very old world,"
said Satie once.
And he never grew up
but was always a child
with an old man's smile.

From his earliest years,
he loved to play music.
He went to a school
to learn how to play and compose.

Throughout his life,
he wanted to make a new kind of music,
a kind of music both very young
and very old, very bold and very shy,
that followed no rules
but its own.

RULES

Satie's music was like an old chant
and wild tunes from kick lines or choruses,
but mixed together. Many did not like it.

Around him was a world of black top hats
and stiff, starched collars
and gloves and bows and curtsies.
It frightened and confused him.
People thought he was mad,
that his music was bad
because it was strange.

So when he was in school
things did not go well.
He dropped out
and then in
and then out.
He did not go back
until he was almost forty.

LE CHAT NOIR

As a young man, he lived in Paris.
He began to make friends.
One was a poet who
worked as a plumber
in his spare time.
He took Satie to a famous café,
the Black Cat, Le Chat Noir,
a café with grand sweeping staircases
and dark wooden chairs
and its very own cat named Maigriou—
and the bones of a poet were hidden inside,
and upstairs was a theater
where people put on plays
with shadow puppets
made of
zinc.

Le Chat Noir—
where all of the poets, the painters,
the actors and dancers,
the wizards and wisecrackers would sit
and sip and scribble ideas or talk about art.
Some of these people were painters of clowns.
Some were inventors of luminous hats,
or schemes to cover the oceans with cork
so they could travel
from New York to France.

It was a good place to be.
It was like a dream.
It was the furthest thing possible
from the world of rules
and polite smiles
and handshakes
and spats
and bowler hats.

Satie was asked to play the piano
at the Black Cat.
Here was a chance
to play his strange music,
his music which sounded
like kick line songs
and ancient chants,
but mixed together.

Here was a chance to have people listen.
At twenty-two
he wrote his most famous
pieces for piano,
the *Gymnopédies*,
which he played
at the Black Cat
while patrons stopped drinking
and stared at the smoke,
while the cat,
who was slinking
across the piano,
was still.

No one could tell
as they heard this soft music
if it was happy or sad,
this music like messages
from a child's dream world.
They sat without moving
at the Black Cat.

Finally
Satie had found friends
who would not laugh
at his strange ways and tunes.
He had found
a home.

Satie wrote songs and composed music for puppet shows.

He wrote ballets for parties and music for magical spells.

Often he would name his pieces things like "The Dreamy Fish,"

or maybe "In a Horse Costume,"

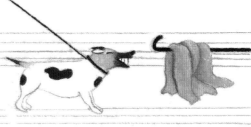

or sometimes "Sketches and Temptations of a Fat Man Made of Wood."

He wrote several "Real Flabby Preludes (for a Dog),"

and a set of seven pieces called "Three Pieces in the Shape of a Pear."

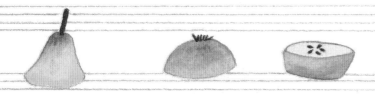

Other composers wrote instructions in their music like

"Fast" or

"Loud" or

"Slowly."

Satie wrote, "From the end of the eyes,"

"In the throat,"

"On yellowing velvet,"

and "I want a hat of solid mahogany."

One day at the Black Cat,
Satie met an artist and model named Suzanne Valadon,
and fell in love with her.
She already had a boyfriend
who was a lawyer,
a very rich man.
Satie didn't mind.
He invited himself along on their dates.

The three of them went together:
the clever young artist,
the penniless musician,
and the wealthy young man,
who was very, very irritated.
When they went to the theater,
Satie hired two boys
to walk in front of them,
banging drums.

But Satie had a temper,
a terrible temper,
and he would often have tantrums
and yell at his friends
for making fun of his music
or liking his music
or breaking his umbrella,
and sometimes he would never speak to them again.

He and Suzanne
argued and argued
one night in his apartment
until finally
he threw her right out the window.

Luckily, she had been
a circus

a c r o b a t

so she sailed lightly
through the air,
landed on her
toes,
and
walked
away
from Erik Satie,
the strange and
obnoxious Erik Satie,
forever.

So it went with Erik Satie:
He made friends and lost them
in starts and in fits.
Erik Satie
walked alone often
through the streets of our world
like a visitor here.
His habits were odd.
He wore seven
identical
gray velvet suits
and that was all.
He did not take baths,
but scraped himself
with a piece of stone.

Satie was very poor.

He had to move into a room so small

that to get through the door,

he had to climb onto his bed.

When he got even poorer

they kicked him out of even this tiny, cold room.

He and a friend

put all of his belongings

in a wheelbarrow

and wheeled them through the streets of Paris

to another apartment

in a different part of town

where he stayed

for the rest of his life.

He had to cover the windows with paper

because the neighbors were always peeking in

to see the strange man,

the man like a child,

who lived next door.

He lived there alone

amidst trash and stacks of paper

and a tuneless and tinny piano.

Satie was poor
because many people
did not like his music.
He had dropped out of school,
so they said he had not learned
the rules
of how to compose.
He realized he had made a mistake.
He needed to know rules
so he could break them.

In 1905,
when he was thirty-nine,
Satie went back to school
to learn music.
He did not complain.
He sat at his desk.
He patiently did homework
and sat with the others,
those half his age.
And he got his degree.

When he graduated,
he dressed like a man in an office.
He always carried an umbrella
and wore a bowler hat,
and looked, people said,
like he could not be
more normal.
And yet
in his eye
there was a strange
glint.

PARADE

In 1917, Erik Satie and his friends
put on a ballet called *Parade*.
Satie wrote the music.
The sets and the costumes
were built and painted
by an artist named Pablo Picasso.
The ballet's story was gripping:
a circus—a thief—and a girl,
a plucky girl with a gun
on a bicycle, shooting—all these
and more, dancing like a film
sped up in a dream.
People were used to ballet
being very polite,
very graceful and dainty.
This
was not
that.

The music for *Parade* was funny
and mechanical.
It sounded like jazz
played on xylophones, typewriters, and sirens.
Some of the dancers had to wear
tall
buildings.

The audience didn't like *Parade* at all.
They thought it was a joke on them.
Maybe it was.
They started to yell and to fight.
The man who had planned the ballet
was attacked
by a woman with a hat pin.

One critic gave it
a very bad review.
Satie was upset.
He had a fit.
He sent the critic a postcard
which said.

Le Carnet
de la
semaine

Sir, dear friend.
You are not only
a butt,
but a butt
without music.

This was not a good idea.
The critic took Satie to court.
Outside the courtroom,
Satie's friends got in a fight with the police.
Satie came very close
to going to jail.

Though Satie got older
he always seemed young.
He wrote other ballets,
each one an experiment
in what music and dancers could do.
In 1924, he wrote *Cancelled*,
a ballet with a movie
that began with Satie and
the painter Picabia,
Francis Picabia,
shooting a cannon
at the audience,
and included a funeral
led by a camel.

On the music was printed:
"When will people get out
of the habit
of explaining everything?"

The hardest thing
about making *Cancelled*,
the ballet with a movie,
was finding a garage
where they could keep
the camel.

On opening night
the lead dancer was so worried
he got sick.
He thought people would hate the ballet
and think it was strange.
He said that he couldn't
dance that night.
The crowds waited eagerly
to get in and see
this odd new ballet.
But it did not open that night.
Traffic was jammed up for blocks.
Luckily, the posters
already said
Cancelled.

It was not cancelled long.
It opened a few days later.
It had a huge audience.
Its sets were made of metal discs.
They showed the movie
of Satie and Picabia
shooting the cannon.
A fireman stood with two buckets of water
while dancers around him spun and twirled.

At the end, no one knew
what they had just seen,
but they knew that they liked it,
and they clapped and they clapped.
Satie and Picabia drove up on the stage
in a small car,
and spun it in circles,
waving and waving
until the applause
stopped.

Shortly afterward, Satie got sick.
He could not stay at home
with no one to take care of him.
So he lay in bed in a hotel room
and the door was attached to him
with string.
His friends came.
Sometimes he yelled at them.
Sometimes he was sorry for things he had done.

He was taken to the hospital,
where the nuns came and went.
On the first of July,
he died.

The day of his funeral
poets, musicians, and artists all came
to the church near his home
to bid him good-bye.
In the chapel a wedding went on
while the body was buried.
Like his music
it was happy and sad
at the same moment,
not one or the other.
That's the way with his pieces:
Sometimes they can sound
like night falling, and darkness;
sometimes they can sound
like him dancing,
strange Mr. Satie,
a child-man dancing
with his umbrella,
joyfully spinning,
and grinning,
alone.

The story of Erik Satie may be strange, but it is true.

Satie's childhood was probably not easy. In 1872, his mother died, and he and his brother were sent to live with his grandparents. He studied music off and on as a teenager, but it didn't go well. He eventually left to join the military, but that didn't work out either. He disliked it so much that he sat outside in the cold night air until he developed bronchitis and was discharged. At this point he moved to Paris and met the poets, musicians, and painters who would become so important to him.

Most of Satie's music was written for piano, such as the *Gymnopédies* (1888), the *Gnossiennes* (1889–1897), and the *Sonatine bureaucratique* (1917). There are some important exceptions, however. One of his most famous pieces is an opera with no action called *Socrate* (1919). And he was the first composer to create Muzak, writing chamber pieces that were supposed to be repeated again and again as "musical wallpaper."

Later in his life, he also wrote several famous scores for ballets—*Parade* (1917), *Les Aventures de Mercure* (1924), and *Relâche* ("Cancelled", 1924). One critic described the bizarre music and costumes for *Parade* as "sur-real"—more than real. Now, whenever we want to say that something is strange to the point of being dreamlike, we call it *surreal*.

In 1925, shortly after the success of these final ballets, Satie got sick and died, most likely of liver problems. His final words were, "Ah! The cows …" No one except Satie had been inside his apartment for almost thirty years. When his friends went in, they found the floor littered with stacks of dirty paper and little cards that advertised magic castles for rent and airships of metal.

Though Satie lived most of his life in poverty and obscurity, his music profoundly affected many famous classical composers—Claude Debussy, Maurice Ravel, Igor Stravinsky, John Cage—and also many composers of jazz. Today, his music is famous, heard in movies and as backgrounds for advertisements. One of his pieces, "Vexations," which is supposed to be repeated eight hundred and forty times, takes over eighteen hours to perform, and appears in the *Guinness Book of World Records*.

Satie was a genius and a crank, a magician and a child, a fool and a visionary, a gentle man with a violent temper, a medieval composer on the cutting edge of modernity.

Satie, most of all, was Satie.

Further reading and listening:

There are several excellent biographies of Erik Satie for adults, but perhaps the best and most interesting sources are the writings of Satie himself and those who knew him: Ornella Volta's *Satie Seen through His Letters* (New York: Marion Boyars, 2000); Robert Orledge's *Satie Remembered* (Portland: Timber Press, 1995); and Ornella Volta's *A Mammal's Notebook: Collected Writings of Erik Satie* (London: Atlas Press, 1996).

Those who wish to listen to Satie's music should perhaps start with some of his most famous piano pieces; the *Gymnopédies*, the *Gnossiennes*, and *Three Pieces in the Shape of a Pear*.

VIKING
Published by Penguin Group
Penguin Young Readers Group, 345 Hudson Street, New York, New York 10014, U.S.A.

First published in 2003 by Viking, a division of Penguin Young Readers Group

1   3   5   7   9   10   8   6   4   2

Text copyright © M. T. Anderson, 2003
Illustrations copyright © Petra Mathers, 2003

LIBRARY OF CONGRESS CATALOGING-IN-PUBLICATION DATA
Anderson, M. T.
Strange Mr. Satie / by M.T. Anderson ; illustrated by Petra Mathers.
p. cm.
Summary: Introduces the life of the French composer, Erik Satie,
who spent his entire career challenging established conventions in music.
ISBN 0-670-03637-4 (hardcover)
1. Satie, Erik, 1866-1925. 2. Composers—Biography—Juvenile literature.
[1. Satie, Erik, 1866-1925. 2. Composers.] I. Mathers, Petra, ill. II. Title.
ML3930.S28A63 2003   780'.92—dc21   2003000949

Printed in the U.S.A.
Set in Weiss

Endpaper text adapted from Erik Satie's *Memoirs of an Amnesiac*

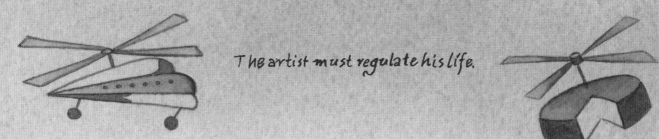

The artist must regulate his life.

Here is a precise schedule of my daily activities:

7:18 a.m.: I get up:

10:23 to 11:47 a.m.: Inspiration.

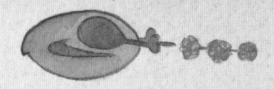

I start lunch at 12:11 and leave the table at 12:14.

13:19 to 14:53 p.m.: A healthy ride on my horse around my estates.

15:12 to 16:07 p.m.: More inspiration.

16:27 to 18:47: Various activities (sword-fighting, reflection, staying still, visits, thinking hard, dexterity, swimming, etc.).

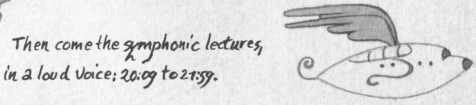

Dinner is served beginning at 19:16 and ending at 19:20.

Then come the symphonic lectures, in a loud voice: 20:09 to 21:59.

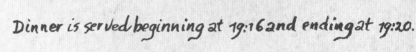

I go to bed regularly at 22:37. Once a week, I wake up with a start at 3:19. That's on Tuesday.

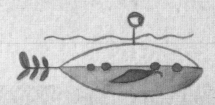